A Child's First Book
—— of ——
·P·R·A·Y·E·R·S·

MARJORIE NEWMAN
Illustrated by Elvira Dadd

Fleming H. Revell Company
Tarrytown, New York

This Book
belongs to

_____

_____

Contents

Myself and My Family

My home can be full of love;
and I can remember that God loves us, too.

God bless all those that I love.
God bless all those that love me.
God bless all those that love
those that I love, and all those
that love those who love me.

New England Sampler

Running, jumping, seeing -
Laughing, skipping - *being*!
I love to be alive!
Thank You, God.

My pets are part of our family, God,
And we are part of Your family.
Please help us to care for animals the way
        You would like us to, so they are happy
        to be living with us.

Dear God
Thank You for grandmothers and grandfathers.
        They've lived longer than me,
        and have lots of things to show me and tell me.
Thank You, too, for babies.
        I've lived longer than them,
        and have lots of things to show them and tell them.
Please help us to be kind to one another,
        and so to have lots of happy times together!

5

Everyday Experiences

There isn't *room* in our house!
We have to share the space,
And sometimes I get very cross -
You can see that by my face!

I'm sorry, God! I wouldn't want
To live here all alone...
But help me, please, to find a spot
To be my very own.

Dear God,
I often wish I had Mum all to myself!
Please help me to be patient when she's busy,
and kind when she's tired.
Thank You for my mum.
And thank You for my dad, too!

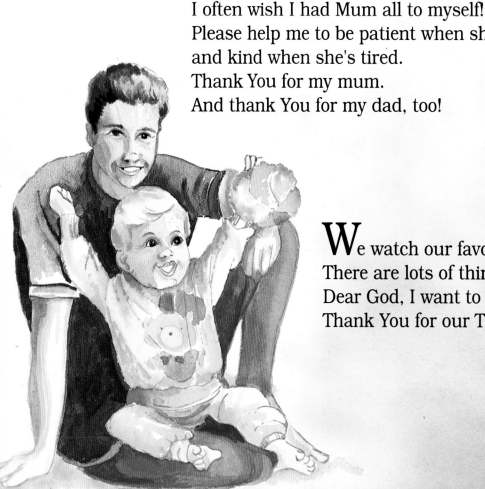

We watch our favourite programmes.
There are lots of things to see.
Dear God, I want to say
Thank You for our T.V.

Dear God,
I love our kitchen!
    I love the smell of cooking, the taste of food,
    and the sound of water swirling in the sink.
I love our sitting room!
    I love the feel of the soft cushions,
    and the sound of Mom and Dad singing to the radio.
I love my bedroom!
    I love to see the starlight from the window.
I love our home! Thank You, God.

At Night

Night is the time when we curl up in bed and go to sleep.
God is still taking care of us!

Good night! Good night!
Far flies the light.
But God's love shall shine above,
Making all bright.
Good night! Good night!

Victor Hugo (translation) 1802–85

Bath and bed and storytime,
A kiss to say goodnight!
Thank You, God, for happy days
And cozy sleep at night.

Jesus, tender Shepherd, hear me,
Bless thy little lamb tonight.
Through the darkness be Thou near me,
Keep me safe till morning light.

Mary Duncan 1814–40

Dear God –
I don't always want to go to bed when Mom says!
Please then help me to think about the fun of bath time!
Please help me to think about tucking happily in bed with my toys.
And please help me to remember – mom gets tired!
Thank you, God, for bedtime.

Lord, when we have not any light
And mothers are asleep,
Then through the stillness
of the night
Thy little children keep.

Annie Matheson 1853–1924

Food

Mealtimes are good! We like to eat and drink –
and we can remember that God planned the world so that things would grow.
We can do our part, too!

We dig the ground,
And sow the seeds,
And watch the rain,
And pull up the weeds,
And feel the sun,
And wait, and wait...
And up come the plants!
Isn't that great!

And when they've grown,
Mom gives a nod -
We pick - and eat!
Oh, thank You, God!

Thank You for the world so sweet,
Thank You for the food we eat.
Thank You for the birds that sing.
Thank You, God, for everything!

E. Rutter Leatham 1870-1933

All good gifts around us
Are sent from Heaven above!
Then thank the Lord, O thank the Lord
For all His love!

Matthias Claudius 1740-1815
Translated by Jane Montgomery Campbell 1817-78

Dear God,
We get very hungry!
Thank You for the things we have to eat –
    like puddings and pies and ice cream!

We get very thirsty!
Thank You for the things we have to drink –
    like juice, and milk, and clear, cool water!

Some children don't get enough.
Please help people to care about them,
    so that they can have more.

Outdoors

It's fun to go outdoors! We can enjoy ourselves -
and we can see the wonders of the world God has made.

It is a good thing to give thanks unto the Lord,
and to sing praises to Your name, O Most High!

Psalm 92:1

Dear Father God, Thank You for making the world.
Please help us to do our share in taking care of it.

For all things fair we hear or see
Father in Heaven, we thank Thee!

Ralph Waldo Emerson 1803-1882

Dear God - I love to go out for walks!
Sometimes I splash through puddles,
and feel the rain on my face!
Sometimes the wind blows, fierce and strong!
Sometimes the sun shines,
and I want to sing and dance under the blue sky!
Sometimes the snow falls,
and I slip and slide and shout!
Father God - I love to go out for walks!

Dear Father, hear and bless
Thy beasts and singing birds.
And guard with tenderness
Small things that have no words.

Anon.

13

Playgroup

It's good to have friends! And when we play with other people
we can remember that God made everyone, and loves us all.

Help us to do the things we should,
To be to others kind and good,
In all we do, in work or play
To grow more loving every day.

Rebecca Weston circa 1890

With my song will I praise Him!

Psalm 28: 7

Dear God,
Thank You for playtimes.
Sometimes all my friends want to do the same thing at the same time!
Then please help us to take turns and share.

I love to make things, God!
Thank You for my hands, and my eyes, and my thinking!
And thank You because You make things, too!

Outings

Outings can be exciting! Visiting people –
going on vacation – riding on a bus or train or plane – going for a walk...
We can discover more of God's world, and see how good it is.

Splashing in the ocean
Digging in the sand
Playing with a beach ball
Walking hand in hand.
Father God, I want to say –
Thank You for our holiday!

With You beside us, Father God,
We journey on our way.
What need we fear, when You are near,
O King of night and day!

St. Columba 521-597 (slightly adapted)

Children laughing
Birds singing
Flowers growing
Trees blowing
Ducks splashing
Kites flying
People walking
Moms talking
Thank You, God, for the park!

If I take the wings of the morning
and dwell in the uttermost parts of the sea,
even there shall Thy hand lead me,
and Thy right hand shall hold me.
Psalm 139:9,10

Rock and highlands,
Wood and island
Praise ye, praise ye
God the Lord!
John Stuart Blackie 1809-95

Not So Well

Sometimes we don't feel well.
But we can say thank You to God for all the people who help to make us feel better –
and we can be sure God loves us, and wants what's best for us.

Thank You, God, for hospitals,
Doctors and nurses too.
Thank You because You'll be with me
Whatever we have to do
To make me feel quite strong and well.
Then what a lot I'll have to tell!

I don't feel so well today, God.
Please help me to feel better soon.

Dear God,
Sometimes people get so old or sick,
        the only way they can be well again
        is to be with You in Heaven.
We are sad they have to leave us.
But we are glad they are all right now;
        and we like to know You have promised
        we shall see them again one day.

Holy God, who madest me,
Make me fit to worship Thee.
Fit to stand, fit to run,
Fit for sorrow, fit for fun.
Fit for work, fit for play,
Fit to face life every day.
Holy God, who madest me
Make me fit to worship Thee.

Anon (slightly adapted)

19

Birthdays

Birthdays are such fun!
It's a good time to remember all the things God has given us!

He cares for you.
1Peter 5:7

I'm a whole year older,
And a whole year taller.
And I can do lots more
Than when I was smaller!
Thank You, God!

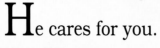

Dear God,
Thank You for our birthdays.
As we grow older,
    please help us to learn more and more about You.
You are with us all through our lives,
    no matter how old we get!

Easter

Easter is a time when we specially think about the Lord Jesus.
We can think about new life, as well – baby chicks and birds
and butterflies, lilies and all the flowers of Easter time.

The world itself keeps Easter Day,
And Easter larks are singing,
And Easter flowers bloom today
And Easter buds are springing!

John Mason Neale 1818-66 (slightly adapted)

On Good Friday we are sad, because Jesus died for us on a cross.
But on Easter Sunday we are glad, because He is alive again!
Thank You, God!

Christmas

Christmas is a very special time!
We celebrate the first Christmas, when – because of God's love for us –
baby Jesus came into the world at Bethlehem.

Glory to God in the highest,
and on earth peace, goodwill toward men.

Luke 2:14

Trees, and stars, and stockings, and toys,
Laughing, and singing, and playing, and noise,
Stories, and presents, and quiet times too,
And everyone happy, and so much to do -
Thank You, God, for Christmas!

Dear God,
Please help us to make as many people happy as we possibly can,
because we're glad baby Jesus was born in Bethlehem
on the first Christmas.

Be near me, Lord Jesus. I ask You to stay
Close by me for ever, and love me, I pray.
Bless all the dear children in Thy tender care,
And fit us for Heaven, to live with Thee there.

Anon.

God bless us, everyone!

Charles Dickens 1812-70

Uncredited prayers are by the author

Copyright © 1991 Hunt and Thorpe
Text © Marjorie Newman
Illustrations © Elvira Dadd
Originally published in the UK by Hunt and Thorpe 1991
First published in North America by Fleming H. Revell Company.
ISBN 0-8007-7129-X

Manufactured in Singapore.